Jackstraws

Other Books by Charles Simic

Jackstraws

Poems

Charles Simic

A Harvest Book
Harcourt, Inc.
SAN DIEGO   NEW YORK   LONDON

Library of Congress Cataloging-in-Publication Data
Simic, Charles, 1938–
Jackstraws: poems/Charles Simic.
p.   cm.
ISBN 0-15-100422-6
ISBN 0-15-601098-4
I. Title.
PS3569.I4725J33   1999
811'.54—dc21   98-35354

Text set in New Baskerville
Designed by Lori McThomas Buley
Printed in the United States of America
First Harvest edition 2000
F E D C B A

this moment—what is it—just
a mosquito, a fly, a speck, a scrap of breath . . .

ADAM ZAGAJEWSKI

Contents

Part I

The Voice at 3 A.M.

Who put canned laughter
Into my crucifixion scene?

Speck-Sized Screaming Head

Hoping to make yourself heard,
Mr. No-See?
Busting your balls
For one long, bloodcurdling scream,
Out of the dustheap
At my feet.

Fat chance. Someone's just putting
A quarter in the jukebox,
Someone else is starting the pink Cadillac convertible
On the street,
And I'm lifting and cocking the broom
In your direction.

The Soul Has Many Brides

In India I was greatly taken up
With a fly in a temple
Which gave me the distinct feeling,
It was possible, just possible,
That we had met before.

Was it in Mexico City?
Climbing the blood-spotted, yellow legs
Of the crucified Christ
While his eyes grew larger and larger.
"May God seat you on the highest throne
Of his invisible Kingdom,"
A blind beggar said to me in English.
He knew what I saw.

At the saloon where Pancho Villa
Fired his revolvers at the ceiling,
On the bare ass of a naked nymph
Stepping out of a lake in a painting,
And now shamelessly crawling up
One of Buddha's nostrils,
Whose smile got even more secretive,
Even more squint-eyed.

The History of Costumes

Top hats and tight-fit monkey suits,
You pointed to the map of the world
With your silver-tipped walking sticks
And fixed my fate forever on a dot.

Already on the very next page,
I saw my white sailor suit parachuting
Among bricks and puffs of smoke
In a building split in half by a bomb,

The smoke that was like the skirts
Slit on the side to give the legs the freedom
To move while dancing the tango
Past ballroom mirrors on page 1944.

Medieval Miniature

Souls burning in hell,
How exceedingly modest your eternal torments
Appear to me in comparison
To that of a firebombed city.

A couple of awkward-looking devils
Are sticking long pitchforks in you.
Another is down on his knees
Reviving the fire by blowing on it.

It's enough to make the sinners go ha-ha,
When in two whoops and a holler
A whole neighborhood can be incinerated
Leaving nothing much to see.

A lone dog roaming in the rubble
Can break the meanest heart.
By the looks of it he's young
And curious. We leave him thus,

Earnestly digging with his paws.
The woman licked by flames
In the meantime has divine breasts.
The unknown artist made sure of that.

Private Eye

To find clues where there are none,
That's my job now, I said to the
Dictionary on my desk. The world beyond
My window has grown illegible,
And so has the clock on the wall.
I may strike a match to orient myself.

In the meantime, there's the heart-
Stopping hush as the building
Empties, the elevators stop running,
The grains of dust stay put.
Hours of quiescent sleuthing
Before the Madonna with the mop

Shuffles down the long corridor
Trying doorknobs, turning mine.
That's just little old me sweating
In the customer's chair, I'll say.
Keep your nose out of it.
I'm not closing up till he breaks.

The Common Insects of North America

Bumble Bee, Soldier Bug, Mormon Cricket,
They are all out there somewhere
In the audience, as it were,
Behind Joe's Garage, in the tall weeds
By the snake handler's church,
On the fringe of a beaver pond.

Painted Beauty is barefoot and recumbent.
Clouded Wood Nymph has been sight-seeing
And has caught a shiver. Book Louse
Is reading about the battle of Gettysburg.
Chinese Mantid is praying again.

Now that Rat Flea is feeling amorous,
Hermit Beetle has elected to play
Sotto voce in the woods. Widow Dragonfly
Doing leg splits could use a pair of
Eentsy-weentsy prescription shades
Before she comes to a dreadful end.

De Occulta Philosophia

Evening sunlight,
Your humble servant
Seeks initiation
Into your occult ways.

Out of the late-summer sky,
Its deepening quiet,
You brought me a summons,
A small share in some large
And obscure knowledge.

Tell me something of your study
Of lengthening shadows,
The blazing windowpanes
Where the soul is turned into light—
Or don't just now.

You have the air of someone
Who prefers to dwell in solitude,
The one who enters, with gravity
Of mien and imposing severity,
A room suddenly rich in enigmas.

Oh supreme unknowable,
The seemingly inviolable reserve
Of your stratagems
Makes me quake at the thought
Of you finding me thus

Seated in a shadowy back room
At the edge of a village
Bloodied by the setting sun,
To tell me so much,
To tell me absolutely nothing.

Live at Club Revolution

Our nation's future's coming into view
With a muffled drumroll
In a slow, absentminded striptease.
Her shoulders are already undraped,
And so is one of her sagging breasts.
The kisses she blows to us
Are as cold as prison walls.

Once we were a large wedding party.
It was a sunny weekend in June.
Women wore flowers on their straw hats
And white gloves over their hands.
Now we run dodging cars on the highway.
The groom, someone points out, looks like
President Lincoln on a death notice.

It's time to burn witches again,
The minister shouts to the congregation
Tossing the Bible to the ceiling.
Are those Corinna Brown's red panties
We see flying through the dark winter trees,
Or merely a lone crow taking home
His portion of the day's roadkill?

Mother Tongue

That's the one the butcher
Wraps in a newspaper
And throws on the rusty scale
Before you take it home

Where a black cat will leap
Off the cold stove
Licking its whiskers
At the sound of her name.

Non-Stop War with Bugs

An ideal hideout under my bed
To make big plans, grow brazen,
Crawl in and out of my nose
As I lie with my eyes tightly shut
Dreaming of a world
Beyond these sad appearances.

Teeny dadaists on the march,
You're sly and most witty
As you disrupt my rare moments
Of calm, making me perform
Showstopping contortions
To reach after you with a slipper
In a fit of unbecoming frenzy.

Midnight Freight

Mannequins once employed to gauge
The effects of the atomic blast
Seated on my living room sofa
Looking like my dead parents
The day they eloped to be married.

There is an old newsreel of them
In the Nevada desert: Dad's tie is askew,
Mother's Sunday hat is about to slip off,
His gray suit and her dress are rumpled,
The two of them are smiling faintly.

By the streetlight on the corner,
I can see their white Buick parked
With its doors thrown wide open.
Three blind mice is what we are
Coming together like this at midnight.

Their heads slumping in reply,
Pressing closer against their hearts'
Heavy silence. It could hardly
Be spoken of, the grand dummy-up
Of it all, and here I keep talking.

Barber College Shave

In my head thrown back as in a nose bleed,
There are, of course,
A dozen or so replicas of myself,
Much reduced, wearing Halloween masks.

They sit at the same long table
Debating with a conspiratorial air
The baffling question of my true identity,
The contradictory evidence

Like a quick shuffle of smutty postcards:
Here he is hanging someone's pink panties
On a gravestone, smoking a cigar in a saloon
In Amarillo, reading philosophy at night,

Asking the executioner how the chair works ...
What the hell is going on here, I shouted,
At which the apprentice barber rushed over
And threw a steaming hot towel over my eyes.

The Street of Martyrs

Catherine, whose neck was broken
On a steering wheel of a Buick convertible
While milk gushed from her breasts.
Max the giant whose mouth is a black cavern
Since his tongue was amputated.
Barbara, whose father kept her in a closet
So no man could see her.
The All-American shortstop whose coffin
He says, will be a matchbox.

They stop strangers on the street
To warn them about sick and injured bugs
They may be stepping on.
If they meet someone with very large ears,
They try to hang their crutches on them.
When it snows, they walk in circles
Making snowflakes sizzle on the tip of their tongues.

Poor Little Devil

He's a devil while his mom's a saint.
He grins in church, looks glum pitching pennies.
Batty schoolgirls bring him candy
Tucked inside their sweatshirts.
Nipples smeared with licorice
For him to lick while his hairy tail
Brushes up against their bare legs.

Defenders of public decency
March and carry signs outside the museum
In which naked Christ hangs on the cross.
It's supposed to make you stop and think.
Indeed, one day walking around the old neighborhood,
I did finally stop and think

About the way they dressed him in a new uniform
With gold buttons and even a medal
So he lay there in the open coffin
Smiling wistfully for his mother.
Poor little devil, the mourners said,
One by one opening their umbrellas
Against something foul about to descend.

Streets Paved with Gold

Our prisons are dangerously overcrowded
And seething with violence, I've read today.
Is that why this small town is so empty?
Store windows with out-of-business signs.
Even the Star Theater is boarded up,
Its marquee blank save for the word MONSTER.

At the diner we heard so much about we found
The lone waitress standing on a chair
Hanging Christmas decorations on a string.
"She's an idealist in an undertaker's shop,"
You whispered as we read the stained menu
Waiting for her to turn and acknowledge us.

"Life in these hinterlands never agrees
With any philosophy of life you or I may have,"
I wanted to say, but it was too cold to speak.
On the street everything had that gray look
One gets for knowing such truths,
And the parking lot was a sheet of black ice.

The Gang of Mirrors

And the one that's got it in for you,
That keeps taunting you
In an old man's morning wheeze
Every time you so much as glance at it,
Or blurt something in your defense,
Screaming, raising your chin high,
While it spits and chokes in reply.

The razor is at your throat.
The lines are inscribing themselves
On your forehead as you listen closely
With a poultice of tissue paper
Already reddening under your left eye.

St. George and the Dragon

When Queen Money
Sits naked in my lap,
And her fat bulldog
Comes to growl

While she rides me
Like a horsey
Using her long red hair
As a whip,

And the ceiling at midday
Is a lush maze
Of tree shadows
Tangling and untangling themselves,

And all that comes to mind
Is St. George rearing up
With a lance to slay
The fire-spitting dragon.

The Famous No-Shows

In small, sunless rooms,
In gray-wall-and-ceiling revery,
I looked for them
Now and then.

Wherever I went
Trouble paid my way,
Like a roadside weed,
I could not be still for a day.

At every step,
A new worry overtook me.
If I locked the door,
There was a loud knock.

A small boy stood there
Watching me fidget.
He would not smile,
No matter what I did.

What a night to be out!
I told the tiger cat
Sleeping among the urns
In the window of a funeral home.

The famous no-shows,
Truth, Justice, and so forth—
All I saw was ghost-faced children
Swarming on every corner.

It must've been Halloween.
One bare-legged girl
Wore a long bridal veil.
Her beau was dressed as a vampire.

"Trick or treat," the turbaned taxi driver
Informed me. And it was true!
The avenue we were zipping along
With its wicked potholes,

Its lights changing red to green,
Made me think of an aviary, the splendor
Of parrots fluttering and screeching
Something I couldn't catch just then.

Bug Doctor

Night visitor, do you know about fear?
Do you shit on the run
When you see my long fingernail
Coming after you?
Are you astounded to be in pain
When they crucify you with pins,
Or when I squeeze you tight
Between a thumb and a forefinger?

Writhing in torment, beating your wings,
Your health is delicate,
And now you can't stop shivering.
I suppose your face is pale,
And lined with worry.
The pointiest pencil-point won't do justice
To the terror in your eyes.

Something in me, too, come to think,
Has a way of cringing low.
The perplexity and serious trouble
You've fallen into are familiar to me.
So, buzz off—or whatever it is
You actually do to get around . . .
And say, Is that a new limp you've got,
Or are you just a bit giddy?

My Friend Someone

By the sudden draft of cool air,
It could be, a door has opened
Somewhere in the evening quiet.
Someone hesitates on the threshold
With a faint smile
Of happy premonition.

On this day without a date,
On a back street, dusky
But for the glow of a TV set
Here and there,
And one lone tree in flower
Trailing a long train
Of white petals and shadows.

Taking a Breather

On the steps of a funeral home,
And now a couple of red-faced pallbearers,
(Or whatever they are),
Want me to get lost—but where?

In the movie theater across the street,
There's a door marked EXIT.
On the screen a windblown tumbleweed
Has stopped for a moment
Before a stage-lit gas pump.

A black robe trails the mopped floor
In the state courthouse.
Two boys have hidden under the bed
In the reformatory.
There's a fellow due to be electrocuted
Tomorrow morning
Who says his steak is overdone.

Striped pants and butter gloves,
Strutting back and forth like crows
Over a fresh roadkill,
Forget it! I'm not budging from here.

Part II

El libro de la sexualidad

The pages of all the books are blank.
The late-night readers at the town library
Make no complaints about that.
They lift their heads solely
To consult the sign commanding silence,
Before they lick their finger,
Look sly, appear to be dozing off,
As they pinch the corner of the paper
Ever-so-carefully,
While turning the heavy page.

In the yellow puddle of light,
Under the lamp with green shade,
The star charts are all white
In the big astronomy atlas
Lying open between my bare arms.
At the checkout desk, the young Betelgeuse
Is painting her lips red
Using my sweating forehead as a mirror.
Her roving tongue
Is a long-tailed comet in the night sky.

Arriving Celebrities

Tragedy and Comedy
Stepping out of a limousine
In ritzy furs,
Diminutive skirts,
Blowing kisses
Left and right.

Bedlam of adoring fans,
Pushing and squeezing,
Hollering for a glimpse,
When—all of a sudden!
A hush.
An all-inclusive clam-up.

Is someone, I inquired
Of my neighbors,
Already lying knifed
On the dance floor
Mouthing the name
We are all straining to overhear?

The towering bodyguards
With shaved heads
And mirror-tinted shades,
Don't hear me right,
Or will not deign
To grant my presence.

Modern Sorcery

You could have been just another maggot
Squirming over history's roadkill.
Instead a witch took pity on you, lucky fellow,
Made you say abracadabra, and much else
You didn't understand
While you held on to the hem of her skirt.

You know neither the place nor the hour
Of your transfiguration.
A kitten lapping a drop of milk
Fallen from the Blessed Virgin's breast
In a church at dawn. That's how it felt:
The two of you kneeling there.

Outside, there was a flash of lighting
Like a tongue passing over a bloody knife,
But you were safe.
Hexed once and for all in her open arms,
Giddy and tickled pink with her sorcery.

Big-Time Wrestling

Something and Nothing battle here.
One we never get to see at all,
The other we watch closely
Changing costumes and masks
In hope it'll add up to something.

Our hearts are spilled popcorn
Under the stomping boots
Of some blond angel indignant
At the slow pace of his own demise
In the arms of nothing-we-can-see.

The heavy silence presiding
Has the air of a bow-tied referee
Occasionally raising a false hand
The color of old ivory. The Exits
Are red with hangman's black curtains.

Ship of Fools

I'm the stowaway in the crow's nest.

My old love letters are the sails,
The ones full of sighs and kisses.

At the Captain's Table a moonfaced nun
Is eating a June bug.

In the sky, a flock of white shirts
Are flying to laundry line in Africa.

The Captain sets his beard on fire.

Through the spying glass, I can see the florist on the
    back of a shark
Bringing a dozen bouquets of white roses.

Mummy's Curse

Befriending an eccentric young woman
The sole resident of a secluded Victorian mansion.
She takes long walks in the evening rain,
And so do I, with my hair full of dead leaves.

In her former life, she was an opera singer.
She remembers the rich Neapolitan pastries,
Points to a bit of fresh whipped cream
Still left in the corner of her lower lip,
Tells me she dragged a wooden cross once
Through a leper town somewhere in India.

I was born in Copenhagen, I confide in turn.
My father was a successful mortician.
My mother never lifted her nose out of a book.
Arthur Schopenhauer ruined our happy home.
Since then, a day doesn't go by without me
Sticking a loaded revolver inside my mouth.

She had walked ahead of me and had turned
Like a lion tamer, towering with a whip in hand.
Luckily, in that moment, the mummy sped by
On a bicycle carrying someone's pizza order
And cursing the mist and the potholes.

The Return of the Invisible Man

The invisible man, it turns out, had a daughter,
Equally ethereal.
He wants to know, have I bumped into her lately?
You bet, I says to him.
She's the one wearing me out
With her vanishing acts,
Her I'll-be-damned reappearances.

An apparition I'll cross the street for
Against the traffic,
The buses and honking cabs about to
Leave me legless, or worse.
Even so, day and night
I'm roaming the city, hearing the tap
Of her spiked heels at midnight.

Tell me, he says to that,
Is she still Daddy's little girl?
And how, I assure him, especially
When she's nothing but a figment
Wearing black lace panties,
Fluffing the fat pillows
And teasing the covers off our bed.

Dream Broker

You may find yourself with my help
Taking small, apprehensive steps
In a cabal of side streets,
Doorways on the lurk, dim store signs.
Insomnia Detective Agency, restorers
Of defaced and mislaid memories,
Are at your discreet service:

Here then are the small beads of rain
Rapping against the windowpane
The day your grandmother died.
Here's the chained dog whipped by a man
In full view of the evening train,

And the girl with a white blindfold
Feeling her way in the empty museum.
You expected her hidden companions
To burst after her merrily,
But nobody did. It got dark
For the saint pierced by arrows
And for you, too, chump,
But nobody else came along.

Odd Sympathies

Your continuous yawning makes
Other late customers yawn.
You can't help it, Miss,
And they can't help it.
You both take leisurely turns.

The women with their nails
And lips painted black,
Their dates in concert
Confounding manners and poise.
Opening their mouths wide.

Such pleasing tongues
In full view,
All the intemperance of the color pink
Previously secreted
Until this rash epidemic.

Amour Fou

Black sorrow running after me
In the street,
Calling me Tom Cat,
Mr. Hot-Nuts.

That's why I break my neck,
Dart left and right
Looking for a hole to hide in,
Pretend I don't know her.

A lovey-dovey, hootchie-kootchie
Kind of sorrow.
The people stopping to watch
Think we are both wacko.

In the Street

He was kneeling down to tie his shoes which she
    mistook for a proposal of marriage.

—Arise, arise, sweet man, she said with tears glistening
    in her eyes while people hurried past as if stung by
    bees.

—We shall spend the day riding in a balloon, she
    announced happily.

—My ears will pop, he objected.

—We'll throw our clothes overboard as we rise higher
    and higher.

—I'll smoke a cigar that may sputter fireworks.

—Don't worry my love, she hugged him. Even where
    the clouds are darkest, I have a secret getaway.

Past the Animal Hospital

Maria, the lovebug, Perez,
In a short red dress the wind peeks under
In a dark doorway
Next to a shop full of dead TV sets
And dead moths.

You were asking her
If she hears the caged dogs
Howling our names?
While her black hair blew over her face,
Back and forth,
Till it got caught in her teeth,
And she said nothing.

Filthy Landscape

The season of lurid wildflowers
Strewn on the meadows
Drunk with kissing
The red-hot summer breezes.

A ditch opens its legs
In the half-undressed orchard
Teeming with foulmouthed birds
And smutty shadows.

Scandalous view of a hilltop
In pink clouds of debauchery.
The sun peeking between them
Now and then like a whoremaster.

Love Poem

Feather duster.
Birdcage made of whispers.
Tail of a black cat.

I'm a child running
With open scissors.
My eyes are bandaged.

You are a heart pounding
In a dark forest.
The shriek from the Ferris wheel.

That's it, *bruja*
With arms akimbo
Stamping your foot.

Night at the fair.
Woodwind band.
Two blind pickpockets in the crowd.

Prison Guards Silhouetted
Against the Sky

I never gave them a thought. Years had gone by.
Many years. I had plenty of other things
To worry about. Today I was in the dentist's chair
When his new assistant walked in
Pretending not to recognize me in the slightest
As I opened my mouth most obediently.

We were necking in some bushes by the riverbank,
And I wanted her to slip off her bra.
The sky was darkening, there was thunder
When she finally did, so that the first large
Raindrop wet one of her brown nipples.

That was nicer than what she did to my mouth now,
While I winced, while I waited for a wink,
A burst of laughter at the memory of the two of us
Buttoning ourselves, running drenched
Past the state prison with its armed guards
Silhouetted in their towers against the sky.

The Blizzard of Love

A pastry chef carrying a lit birthday cake
Found himself in a blinding snowstorm.
He met a bride shop saleslady
Modeling one of her feathery dresses.
He met a waiter with a napkin over his arm.

"Why don't you marry the two of us?"
He called after the waiter,
But the heavy flakes hid the blushing bride
And the man in black
Before either one of them had time to reply.

The Once-Over

Slaves of fatality, at times you remember
Your childhood and in the very next breath
Your death comes into view
In a setting so familiar, it could be this house,
This room, this open window.

A bluejay is screeching in the yard.
You turn your head and continue to listen
Long after the danger is over.
The only sound now is that of a caterpillar
Crawling up the window screen.

The scent of lilacs overpowering,
And then as suddenly all gone ...
You open your eyes with a start.
The wall before you like a movie screen
With the grainy old film noir over.

Jackstraws

My shadow and your shadow on the wall
Caught with arms raised
In display of exaggerated alarm,
Now that even a whisper, even a breath
Will upset the remaining straws
Still standing on the table

In the circle of yellow lamplight,
These few roof-beams and columns
Of what could be a Mogul Emperor's palace.
The Prince chews his long nails,
The Princess lowers her green eyelids.
They both smoke too much,
Never go to bed before daybreak.

Beauty Parlor

School of the deaf with a playground
In a tangle of dead weeds and trash
On a street of torched cars and vans,
Here then is the white and red banner,
Grime-streaked and wind-torn,
Still inviting us to the GRAND OPENING.

The one with a flamethrower hairdo
Who set all our hearts on fire,
Where is she today? I inquired
Of a ragged little tree in front,
While its branches took swipes at my head
As if to knock some sense into me.

My Little Utopia

Why the high, wrought-iron fence
With sharp spikes
And the four padlocks and a chain
Over the heavy gate?

I drop by in late afternoon,
Make sure it's locked,
And peek through the bars
At the rows of sunny flowers,

The tree-lined winding path
Already streaked with shadow,
Masking a couple kissing
As they mosey away from me.

Part III

School for Visionaries

The teacher sits with eyes closed.
When you play chess alone it's always your move.
I'm in the last row with a firefly in the palm of my hand.
The girl with red braids, who saw the girl with red braids?

—⁊⁊—

Do you believe in something truer than truth?
Do you prick your ears even when you know damn well
    no one is coming?
Does that explain the lines on your forehead?
Your invisible friend, what happened to her?

—⁊⁊—

The rushing wind slides to a stop to listen.
The prisoner opens the thick dictionary lying on his knees.
The floor is cold and his feet are bare.
A chew-toy of the gods, is that him?

—⁊⁊—

Do you stare and stare at every black windowpane
As if it were a photo of your unsmiling parents?
Are you homesick for the house of cards?
The sad late-night cough, is it yours?

Ambiguity's Wedding

for E.D.

Bride of Awe, all that's left for us
Are vestiges of a feast table,
Levitating champagne glasses
In the hands of the erased millions.

Mr. So-and-So, the bridegroom
Of absent looks, lost looks,
The pale reporter from the awful doors
Before our identity was leased.

At night's delicious close,
A few avatars of mystery still about,
The spider at his trade,
The print of his vermillion foot on my hand.

A faded woman in sallow dress
Gravely smudged, her shadow on the wall
Becoming visible, a wintry shadow
Quieter than sleep.

Soul, take thy risk.
There where your words and thoughts
Come to a stop,
Encipher me thus, in marriage.

On a Lack of Respect Paid to the Ceiling

All of you bummed out and in a deep funk.
Ornery, spiteful mopes
With your noses dragging the floor,
You're not giving proper reverence and esteem
To the imperious, the ever-looming,
Rarely remembered and scrutinized
Overseer of all your goings-on.

There may be a green dragonfly just now
Consulting its dainty shadow,
The excited movement of leaves,
The mystery of light changing?
Or there may be nothing there to see.
Note, please, how quiet the world gets
When you roll your eyes back and look.

Vacant Rooms

Unused to the sound of a voice.
Emptied and swept clean,
Their windows like eyeglasses
Raised to the light
With no one squinting behind them.

Windows spattered with drops of rain
Which take turns listening
To each other fall intermittently
As they go around collecting memories
That do not belong to them,

In a room darkening with shadows
That appear lost, digging deeper
In their pockets for the address
And finding only more shadow,
More silence smudging like ink.

Starless evening: a lamp lit below
By someone as secluded as you,
Who taps her forehead
On the windowpane, visibly troubled
As if overtaken by vertigo.

There's no likelihood she suspects
You are spying on her,
So how is it that she looks up
Now and then and remains looking
At the rows of black windows

As if there were sunset fires
Smoldering in one of them,
Night birds flying to and fro,
A white cat pausing on the parapet,
Its tail a question mark?

The Invisibles

A true detective story
In which a large black dog
Listens at a keyhole
In a room across the way.

Late in the day.
Sunday in May kind of quiet.
Not much to think or say.
The dog still there.

Their window open wide
Despite the drops of rain.
Silent drops,
Blurring my windowpane.

Insomniacs' Debating Society

Our heads like stacks
Of empties.
All night long arguing
Back and forth
With a dripping faucet.

Each drop
Upon close inspection
Baffling,
Gives us a fish-eye
In return.

Every wince
Having the desired effect.
Something adamant
About it,
Something incontrovertible,

Like overhearing
The infinite universe
Tapping its one thought
With a blindman's
Long white cane.

The cueball Buddhist
Among us
Pooh-poohing all foregoing,
Claiming,
It's just our imagination.
Imagine that?

Ancient Divinities

They've got the usual excuses:
We saw it coming, they remind each other.
The new rationality inspired by geometry
Did us in. Immortality is not worth
The price you pay in ridicule, darling.

A late-night chitchat of drag queens
With me eavesdropping at the next table.
Oh the lost world of Eleusinian mysteries!
I feel like I'm wearing a cowbell,
Said the one with long black fingernails
Raising her wineglass in a toast
And acknowledging me with a wink.

The dinner special was Yankee Pot Roast,
Followed by a lot more beer and wine.
And for distraction, while sitting
With nothing further left to say:
A napkin bloodied by fresh lipstick,
A wingless fly trying to crawl under it.

Empty Picture Frame

I meet you everywhere endeavoring to frame
A modest portion of His immensity,
Meaning, I suppose, a lot of sky
Of the cloudless and blue variety,
Over the old cemetery, for instance,
Or over the new town dump
With a field and three scarecrows beyond.

One of them could be that German monk, Eckhart,
Saying: "If a fellow is looking for nothing,
What right has he to complain if he finds nothing?"
True. There was not even a single blackbird
Keeping an eye on the young corn,
So we boosted the frame a bit higher
To where the silence tells all.

Midsummer Feast

for MICHAEL FERBER

Here I am then, nearly blind in both eyes,
Half-deaf, half-lame,
Touched in the head, frothing at the mouth,
A fearful, shrinking worm
Crawling in your carcass, oh mystery,
Raising hell, chewing you out.

My hunch is, you prefer to remain forever
Unthinkable and unsayable,
Merely delectable, so that I may continue
To sate myself on your sweet appearances,
Your luscious, flower-strewn meadows,
Your vast banquets of evening stars.

Obscurely Occupied

You are the Lord of the maimed,
The one bled and crucified
In a cellar of some prison
Over which the day is breaking.

You inspect the latest refinements
Of cruelty. You may even kneel
Down in wonder. They know
Their business, these grim fellows

Whose wives and mothers rise
For the early Mass. You, yourself,
Must hurry back through the snow
Before they find your rightful

Place on the cross vacated,
The few candles burning higher
In your terrifying absence
Under the darkly magnified dome.

House of Horrors

Infinity devours us, folks,
Ah, the screams, the burst of giggles,
The stink of deep-fry,
The taste of candied apples!

The beast with serene table manners
Is behind that white curtain.
The thin knife and fork it uses
Silhouetted stabbing a heart.

And now the public announcement
With the name of lost children.
Don't their parents know
How to mind the little brats?

Or so I shouted into the echoing,
They-are-playing-me-for-a-sucker-
and-it's-been-going-on-forever,
Mostly empty House of Horrors.

To the One Upstairs

Boss of all bosses of the universe.
Mr. know-it-all, wheeler-dealer, wire-puller,
And whatever else you're good at.
Go ahead, shuffle your zeros tonight.
Dip in ink the comets' tails.
Staple the night with starlight.

You'd be better off reading coffee dregs,
Thumbing the pages of the Farmer's Almanac.
But no! You love to put on airs,
And cultivate your famous serenity
While you sit behind your big desk
With zilch in your in-tray, zilch
In your out-tray,
And all of eternity spread around you.

Doesn't it give you the creeps
To hear them begging you on their knees,
Sputtering endearments,
As if you were an inflatable, life-size doll?
Tell them to button up and go to bed.
Stop pretending you're too busy to take notice.

Your hands are empty and so are your eyes.
There's nothing to put your signature to,
Even if you knew your own name,
Or believed the ones I keep inventing,
As I scribble this note to you in the dark.

Head of a Doll

Whose demon are you,
Whose god? I asked
Of the painted mouth
Half buried in the sand.

A brooding gull
Made a brief assessment,
And tiptoed away
Nodding to himself.

At dusk a firefly or two
Dowsed its eye pits.
And later, toward midnight,
I even heard mice.

On the Meadow

With the wind gusting so wildly,
So unpredictably,
I'm willing to bet one or two ants
May have tumbled on their backs
As we sit here on the porch.

Their feet are pedaling
Imaginary bicycles.
It's a battle of wits against
Various physical laws,
Plus Fate, plus—
So-what-else-is-new?

Wondering if anyone's coming to their aid
Bringing cake crumbs,
Miniature editions of the Bible,
A lost thread or two
Cleverly tied end to end.

Empty Rocking Chair

Talking to yourself on the front porch
As the night blew in
Cold and starless.

Everybody's in harm's way,
I heard you say,
While a caterpillar squirmed
And oozed a pool of black liquid
At your feet.

You turned that notion
Over and over
Until your wooden teeth
Clamped shut.

Three Photographs

I could've been that kid
In the old high school photograph
I found in a junk shop,
His guileless face circled in black.

In another, there was a view of Brooklyn Bridge
And a tenement roof with pigeons flying
And boys with long poles
Reaching after them into the stormy sky.

In the third, I saw an old man kneeling
With a mouth full of pins
Before a tall, headless woman in white.

I had no money and it was closing time.
I was feeling my way uncertainly
Toward the exit in the evening darkness.

The Mouse in the Radio

After the late, late news,
You plucked up courage
To scratch a few times
On the wall of your hideaway.

Now that the lights are out,
Feeling the cold,
The bleak solitude,
And so sending out a query,

Or perhaps a heartfelt greeting?
On this starless,
Dateless and otherwise
Largely pitiless night.

The Toy

The brightly painted horse
Had a boy's face,
And four small wheels
Under his feet,

Plus a long string
To pull him this way and that
Across the floor,
Should you care to.

A string in-waiting
That slipped away
With many wiles
From each and every try.

Knock and they'll answer,
My mother told me,
So I climbed the four flights
And went in unannounced.

And found the small toy horse
For the taking

In the ensuing emptiness
And the fading daylight
That still gives me a shudder
As I if I held in my hand
The key to mysteries.

Where is the Lost and Found
And the quiet entry,
The undeveloped film
Of the few clear moments
Of our blurred lives.

Where's the drop of blood
And the tiny nail
That pricked my finger
As I bent down to touch the toy,
And caught its eye?

Wintry light,
My memories are
Steep stairwells
In dusty buildings
On dead-end streets,

Where I talk to the walls
And closed doors
As if they understood me.

—ɷ—

The wooden toy sitting pretty.

No, quieter than that.

Like the sound of eyebrows
Raised by a villain
In a silent movie.

Psst, someone said behind my back.

Talking to the Ceiling

The moths rustle the pages of the evening papers.

A beautiful sleepwalker terrorizes Kansas.

Cannibal waiter ate two of his diners tonight.

I was snooping on myself, pointing the long finger.

Whose orange hairpiece is that, the cop said?

All of creation, you are in my bad books.

In the meantime, I'm always thinking of you Margie.

If only I had a paper crown on my head.

I'd play tapes of your inspired snoring.

The big question, can we continue

To keep the grim reaper laughing?

The long menu of mouthwatering misfortunes

Lies scrawled in the palms of our hands.

Unknown namesake in a roach motel, go to sleep.

Please cut the cards again with eyes closed.

A hundred horror films are crammed in my head.

A baby, you say, smuggled inside a watermelon.

Madame Zaza, come to think, stays open late.

Hangman's convention: ropemaker's workshop.

Do you have fears you'll be crushed by an ant?

In Charon's ferryboat I aim to give ladies my seat.

It's just the way I've been brought up.

Mr. Salesman, would these shoes look good in my
   coffin?

The masked intruder with a dollhouse knife was her!

Next time, I'll try going beddie-bye in a saddle.

Naked truth, you've got to see the boobs on her!

In my youth boys used to light farts in the dark.

The insomniac's brain is a choo-choo train.

Cassandra with a plastic rose between her teeth.

Is this then the cabinet of Dr. Caligari?

Who is that milking a black goat under the blanket?

Like a master criminal dodging his sleeplessness

I sleep in a different bed every night.

John Calvin, stick to your knitting!

My uncle, the general, never came out of the closet

Because he could not find his beach ball.

My love's ill luck was in love with my ill luck.

The goldfish helped me through many a bad night.

Hair by hair we were circumnavigating my head.

I've heard I've been made the official match vendor

Of the great dark night of the soul?

Waiting for the sunrise, the pink birthday cake!

The hurricane century tossed my bed around.

Two tumbleweeds on a pillow, we raced for cover.

We had our candlelight dinner in the Nevada desert.

Here, throw my red hat into the lion cage,

The lady in the zoo said to her crying son.

Oh, to press the chimney to my heart on a windy day!

The air sultry, ice melting in the glasses.

My clock belonged to Queen Persephone herself.

She spent her nights stuffing anchovies into olives.

Coming down from the trees was a big mistake.

The colonel praised the moderate use of electric shocks.

Selling sticks of gum door-to-door in my old age.

Small-beer metaphysician, King of birdshit!

I growled at the mirror till it turned its back on me.

The pitcher on TV stopped in the middle of his windup.

When I toss and turn and bump my head against the wall,

I am the first to offer sincere apologies.

The undercover agent under my covers stayed hidden.

To pass the time, I played a teentsy fiddle

Using one of my love's long black eyelashes as a bow.

Remember me folks as the former target of spitballs.

Girls were already thumbing their noses at me in 1944.

Oh memory, making us all get out and push your hearse!

In calmest tones, I inquired about hell's cuisine

From the worm endeavoring to crawl inside my ear.

A dive with dim lights and middle-aged waitress.

She kept writing my order in elaborate scrawl

Till the clock coughed up its first drop of blood.

Memory, all-night's bedside tattoo artist.

Tell them Death, tell them that yourself.

On the gallows I'll be offering to pick up the check.

Quick, a telescope for a peek inside my head!

Murk extraordinaire, flying rat heaven.

Pray to chance Simic, the jokester in the deck!

And what exactly are these noises in my ear?

Her last lover hid under the bed for years

While she kept a quiet, shady armpit and crotch

For me to snuggle in after lunch in the garden.

And to think, I once rode the dragon-headed ship

On the merry-go-round in the heart of Texas!

Eternity, dim-lit hallway in a skid-row hotel,

My future is my past, the scratchy record sang.

—≈—

Father of the universe, what wine do you sip?

With tiny love bites she ate my heart.

Didn't want the salt and pepper I offered.

Long hours of the night; St. John of the Cross

And Blaise Pascal the cops in a patrol car.

Do you have a favorite black hole in heaven?

The fleeting moments know no care.

Every day I discover serious new obstacles

To my guaranteed pursuit of happiness.

There was a funeral in my coffee cup tonight.

I'm not just any black flea on your ass,

I shouted to every god and devil I could think of!

Infinity's ink has spilled over me

And left me and my bed badly smudged.

—∞—

What could be causing all this. Madam and sir?

The old blues, the kind you never lose.

I'm just a poor, poor boy a long way from home.

Prison and orphanage gave me the shoes I wear.

My love, feeling around for a lost hairpin,

I can imagine you smiling at my nonsense

There are hundreds of flyers on the floor

Addressed to the Occupant.

There are a million zeros crowding for warmth

Inside my head and making it so heavy.

Do you hear them adding and subtracting in the dark?

The one called Jesus coming scared

To ask to sleep in a murderer's bed.

Little rain, keep on falling softly.

Mystic Life

lifetime's solitary thread
for CHARLES WRIGHT

It's like fishing in the dark,
If you ask me:
Our thoughts are the hooks,
Our hearts the raw bait.

We cast the line over our heads,
Past all believing,
Into the starless midnight sky,
Until it's lost to sight.

The line's long unravelling
Rising in our throats like a sigh
Of a long-day's weariness,
Soul-searching and revery

—m—

One little thought against
The supreme unthinkable.

How about that?

Mr. Looney Tunes fishing in the dark
Out of an empty sleeve
With a mourning band on it.

The fly and the spider on the ceiling
Looking on, brother.

—∽—

In the highest school of hide-and-seek,

In its vast classroom
Of smoke and mirrors,
Where we are the twin dunces
Left standing in
The darkest corner.

Our fates in the silence of a mouth
Of the one
Who hath no image,
Glistening there
As if moistened by his tongue.

—∽—

It takes a tiny nibble
From time to time.

Don't you believe it.

It sends a shiver down our spines
In response.

Like hell it does.

There's a door you've never noticed before
Left ajar in your room.

Don't kid yourself.

The song said: *Do nothing*
Till you hear from me.

Yes, of course.

In the meantime,

Wear mirror-tinted
Glasses to bed
Say in your prayers:
In that thou hast sought me,
Thou hast already found me.

That's what the leaves are
All upset about tonight.

Solitary fishermen
Lining up like zeros—

To infinity.

Lying in the shade
Chewing on the bitter verb
"To be."
The ripple of the abyss
Closing in on them.

Therein the mystery
And the pity.

The hook left dangling
In the Great "Nothing,"

Surely snipped off
BY XXXXXX's own
Moustache-trimming scissors . . .

Nevertheless, aloft,

White shirttails and all—

I'll be damned!

SOME OF THESE poems have previously appeared in the following magazines, to whose editors grateful acknowledgment is made: *The New Yorker, The Times Literary Supplement, Harvard Review, Poetry, The London Review of Books, The Michigan Quarterly Review, Boulevard, Yale Review, Raritan Boston Review, Kenyon Review, American Poetry Review, Field, Notre Dame Review, Poetry International, Gettysburg Review, Heat, Vox, Descant, The Georgia Review, The Southern Review,* and *The Exchange.*